Saguaro Cactus

by Conrad J. Storad
photographs by Paula Jansen

 Lerner P   Iinneapolis, Minnesota

For my nieces, Crystal, Brittany, Stephanie, Jenna, Tricia, and Carly. May you always enjoy learning and exploring through the world of books.

—CJS

To David, Ian, and Hali. May we always enjoy the wonders of the earth together.

—PJ

Thanks to our series consultant, Sharyn Fenwick, elementary science/math specialist. Mrs. Fenwick was the winner of the National Science Teachers Association 1991 Distinguished Teaching Award. She also was the recipient of the Presidential Award for Excellence in Math and Science Teaching, representing the state of Minnesota at the elementary level in 1992. Special thanks to our young helpers Sam Kelley and Ben Liestman.

Early Bird Nature Books were conceptualized by Ruth Berman and designed by Steve Foley. Series editor is Joelle Riley.

Lerner Publications Company
A division of Lerner Publishing Group
241 First Avenue North
Minneapolis, Minnesota 55401 U.S.A.

Website address: www.lernerbooks.com

Library of Congress Cataloging-in-Publication Data

Storad, Conrad J.
    Saguaro cactus / by Conrad J. Storad ; photographs by
Paula Jansen.
        p. cm. — (Early bird nature books)
    Includes index.
    ISBN 0-8225-3002-3 (lib. bdg. : alk. paper)
    1. Saguaro—Juvenile literature. 2. Saguaro—Sonoran
Desert—Juvenile literature. [1. Saguaro. 2. Cactus.] I. Jansen,
Paula, ill. II. Title. III. Series
QK495.C11S657 1994
583'.47—dc20   93-38913

Manufactured in the United States of America
3 4 5 6 7 8 – JR – 07 06 05 04 03 02

Contents

The saguaro (suh-WAHR-oh) cactus grows in parts of Arizona and Mexico. The green area shows exactly where saguaros live.

CANADA

UNITED STATES

MEXICO

Be a Word Detective

Can you find these words as you read about the saguaro cactus's life? Be a detective and try to figure out what they mean. You can turn to the glossary on page 47 for help.

carbon dioxide	**photosynthesis**	**seedling**
chlorophyll	**pleats**	**sprout**
nectar	**pollen**	**succulents**
oxygen	**pollinating**	**transpiration**

There is more than one way to form plurals of some words. The word "cactus" has three plural forms—cacti, cactuses, or simply cactus. In this book, we use the plural form "cactuses."

Chapter 1

Some cactuses grow into shapes that look funny. Where do you think you would find a cactus that looks like this?

What Is a Cactus?

Plants are found everywhere on earth. They have been around for billions of years. In fact, plants were here long before the dinosaurs were. One of the most unusual kinds of plants is the cactus.

The cactus belongs to a group of plants called succulents (SUHK-yuh-lehnts). Succulents have special roots, stems, or leaves that soak up and store water. They grow well in places where it doesn't rain very often. That's why they usually are found in deserts.

The cactus is a succulent that stores water in its stem.

Still, cactus plants live in other places besides deserts. More than 2,000 different kinds of cactuses live in North and South America. Wherever they live, all cactus plants are the same in special ways.

The saguaro's scientific name is Carnegiea gigantea. *These are Latin words that mean gigantic candle.*

Spines make shadows on a cactus, helping it stay cool in the hot desert.

The word *cactus* comes from a Greek word that means "thistle." A thistle is a plant with sharp, prickly leaves. Cactus plants do not have leaves. Instead, all cactuses have sharp, pointy spines.

Cactus plants can be many different shapes and sizes. Some are short and round like barrels. Some are tall and skinny like the pipes of a church organ. Others look like piles of flat, prickly pads. Still others grow into big clumps of thick, spiny branches shaped like sausages.

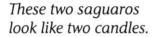

These two saguaros look like two candles.

But the biggest cactus of all is the giant saguaro (suh-WAHR-oh) cactus. The only place you will find saguaros is in the Sonoran Desert. The Sonoran Desert is in southern Arizona and northern Mexico.

Saguaros are giants of the desert.

This is one of the very big and old saguaros that is called Grandaddy.

The giant saguaro cactus can grow to be taller than a four-story building. That's about 50 feet tall! A fully grown saguaro cactus can weigh about as much as five cars—that's 8 tons. And the giant cactus can live for hundreds of years. One giant saguaro named Grandaddy lives in the desert near Tucson, Arizona.

Scientists think that Grandaddy is over 300 years old. Grandaddy is over 40 feet tall. But not every saguaro cactus grows to be as big as Grandaddy.

Birds and other animals drill holes and make their homes in saguaros.

The adult saguaros grow best on hills where they get plenty of sun and warmth. They grow well in the desert's rocky soils. But the saguaros need to begin life in a shady spot. Saguaro seeds sprout only when they land beneath a paloverde (pah-loh-VAIR-day) tree or a creosote (KREE-uh-soht) bush.

Only 1 out of 1,000 saguaro seeds will sprout.

Only 1 out of 500,000 saguaro seeds will become a fully grown cactus. This seedling is about six years old.

When a saguaro seed does sprout, it grows into a tiny plant called a seedling. The seedling pushes its way up through the soil to find sunlight. All plants need sunlight to help them live. The young seedling grows very, very slowly. After a whole year, it still might be shorter than the eraser on your pencil.

Two saguaros grow under the branches of a paloverde tree.

The paloverde tree or creosote bush acts like a nurse to the tiny seedling. It shades the seedling from the strong desert sun. But enough sunlight gets through its branches for the seedling to grow. The nurse plant also hides the seedling from hungry animals. Jackrabbits and squirrels try to nibble chunks from the cactus's soft green stem. But the seedling's sharp spines keep animals from chewing off large pieces.

Sharp spines keep animals like this deer from rubbing against a saguaro cactus and knocking it over.

Chapter 3

Both the bird who built this nest and the saguaro cactus need water to live and grow. How deep into the ground do the saguaro's roots grow to get water?

Water for Life

The saguaro needs water to live and grow. In the desert, plants must work for every drop they get. The growing saguaro has a large tangle of roots. The roots grow only a few inches below the ground. They snake out in all directions around the plant like a giant upside-down umbrella. The roots spread out as wide as the plant is tall. When rain falls, the cactus roots soak up as much water as they can.

The saguaro's roots are short compared to its height, as you can see by looking at one that has fallen over.

A fully grown saguaro cactus can hold enough water to fill 1,000 bathtubs. Like people saving money in a bank, the saguaro stores water for the dry days ahead. The cactus can live for years on this water.

Part of this cactus is swollen with water. Saguaros also grow new arms to store extra water.

The dark part of this fallen saguaro is where water was stored when the cactus was still alive.

The saguaro stores the water inside its large, fleshy stem. Inside the stem are sacks, or pleats, that look like an accordion. As the cactus drinks, the pleats swell with the water. Sometimes the cactus soaks up so much water that it bursts. As the cactus uses stored water during dry times, the pleats shrink.

Chapter 4

Green plants, like saguaros, need water and food to live. What do you think makes plants green?

Food for Growth

A saguaro needs water and food to keep growing. It makes its own food using water soaked up from the soil and carbon dioxide (dy-AHK-side). Carbon dioxide is a gas in the air.

The water travels upward into the plant's thick stem. Carbon dioxide enters the cactus's stem. The stem is where chlorophyll (KLOR-uh-fihl) is stored. Chlorophyll makes plants green. Chlorophyll also turns sunlight into energy.

Like all green plants, saguaros use sunlight, water, carbon dioxide, and chlorophyll to make food for themselves.

With this energy, chlorophyll changes carbon dioxide and water into food for the cactus. This way of making food is called photosynthesis (foh-toh-SIHN-thuh sihs). All green plants make food through photosynthesis.

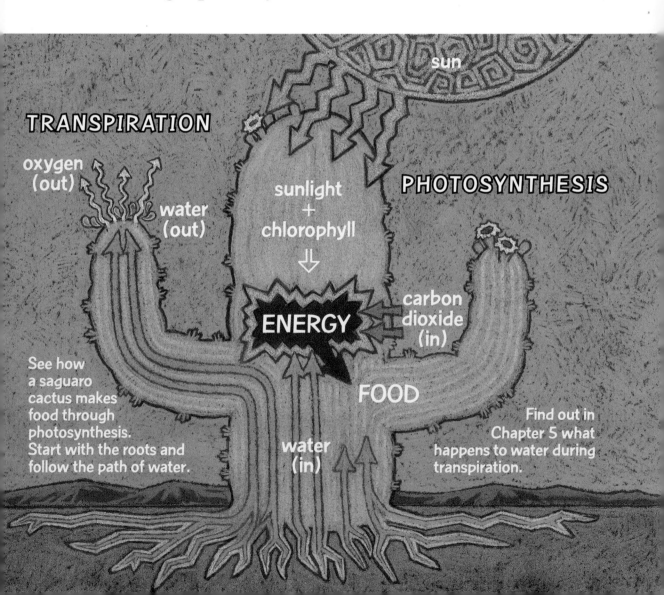

sun

TRANSPIRATION

PHOTOSYNTHESIS

oxygen (out)

water (out)

sunlight + chlorophyll ⬇

ENERGY

carbon dioxide (in)

FOOD

water (in)

See how a saguaro cactus makes food through photosynthesis. Start with the roots and follow the path of water.

Find out in Chapter 5 what happens to water during transpiration.

Chapter 5

The Papago Indians were the first to use a tool made from a saguaro to pick fruit. But the saguaro is giving this person something else besides its fruit. Do you know what it is?

Do Plants Sweat?

Hand in hand with photosynthesis is transpiration (trans-puh-RAY-shun). During photosynthesis, plants take in the gas carbon dioxide. When plants transpire, they give off a gas called oxygen (AHKS-uh-jihn).

The saguaro's thick, waxy skin keeps most of the water inside the cactus.

Breathing is the opposite of transpiration. When people breathe, we breathe in oxygen and breathe out carbon dioxide. How perfect! We give plants carbon dioxide, the gas they need. And plants give us oxygen, the gas we need.

During photosynthesis, plants take in water. When plants transpire, they give off water. The saguaro cactus has a thick, waxy skin. This skin keeps the cactus from losing too much water.

Some large plants can lose enough water through their leaves and stem each day to fill two large bathtubs. That's about 100 gallons of water. A saguaro cactus loses only about one glassful of water each day through transpiration.

Each day, this giant redwood tree can lose enough water through its leaves to fill two large bathtubs.

Chapter 6

Saguaros grow faster when it rains a lot. Can you guess the age of some of these saguaros?

A Saguaro Grows Up

How quickly a saguaro grows toward the sky depends on when it rains and how much it rains. When saguaros are 10 years old, they are only 4 or 5 inches tall. After 25 years, they might stand 2 or 3 feet high. After 50 years, the saguaros are 6 or 7 feet tall. And after 100 years, they might be 35 feet tall. Finally, over another 100 years, saguaros can grow into 50-foot towers.

A 200-year-old saguaro has many arms and is about 50 feet tall. The saguaro grows to be so tall that people need a special tool to help them pick the saguaro's fruits.

The saguaro cactus slowly changes shape as it grows. Very young saguaros look like tiny baseball bats. As they get older, the growing cactuses begin to look more like bowling pins. After 50 years, the cactuses begin to look

A saguaro grows its first arm when it is 60 years old.

As the saguaro grows older, it also grows more and more arms.

like giant candles. In another 10 years, they might sprout their first arm. Arms store extra water. After 100 years, saguaro cactuses have several arms. When saguaros are 200 years old, they have lots and lots of arms.

Chapter 7

At about the same time a saguaro grows its first arm, flowers bloom for the first time. How long is each flower in bloom?

How Seeds Are Made

Flowers and fruits appear for the first time when a saguaro is 60 years old. A large saguaro might have as many as 100 creamy white flowers. Flowers open every night for up to six weeks in May and June. Each flower blooms for only one full night and day.

At night, the flowers' powerful, sweet scent attracts long-nosed bats and moths. During the day, birds and honeybees come to feed on the nectar. Nectar is a sweet juice in flowers. The small animals drinking nectar get covered with pollen. Pollen is the yellow dust that is needed to make seeds. Bats, bees, and other kinds of animals are drinking nectar for themselves.

During the day, honeybees drink sweet nectar from the saguaro's flowers.

They are pollinating (PAHL-uh-nay-ting) the saguaros by carrying pollen from one flower to another. When saguaros are pollinated, seeds begin to grow. The fruit grows around the

Yellow pollen is all over this saguaro flower.

At first, the saguaro fruit is green. It turns bright red when it is ripe and ready to be eaten.

seeds. When animals—even people—eat the ripe fruit, the seeds may be carried to other areas. New plants grow from these seeds, starting the cycle all over again.

Chapter 8

Inside an adult saguaro are strong wood ribs. How do they help the cactus?

The End of Life—Or Is It the Beginning?

A saguaro cactus is not a tree. But part of it is made of wood. Inside a fully grown saguaro are 17 to 28 strong wood rods. These rods form a rib cage in the shape of a circle.

38

They help keep the plant standing. And they keep the saguaro from breaking under the weight of all its stored water. The hard wood from dead saguaros makes excellent building material. The Papago Indian people used saguaro wood to build fences for their animals and furniture for themselves.

Saguaro wood makes strong fences.

The saguaro cactus can live for hundreds of years. But it does not live forever. A strong wind can blow down a tall cactus.

This saguaro is hundreds of years old. People think it is dying because it froze during the winter.

This saguaro cactus has died. It fell to the ground with a huge thud.

Lightning might strike the giant during a desert thunderstorm. If it gets too cold, a saguaro can freeze and die.

Right: *The cactus on the right has died. All that is left are the wood ribs.*

Below: *Some birds drill holes in saguaros to make a nest. The saguaro becomes hard around the hole. When the saguaro dies, the nest falls to the ground. Some people think it looks like a boot.*

When it dies, the giant saguaro is like a hotel to the animals of the desert. Spiders, caterpillars, lizards, snakes, mice, and all kinds of birds live in its broken arms. Soon, nothing is left of the saguaro but its woody ribs. But even while ribs of a dead saguaro lie drying in the sun, a new tiny black seed is sprouting beneath a shady paloverde tree.

The dry ribs of a dead saguaro lie on the ground.

On Sharing a Book

As you know, adults greatly influence a child's attitude toward reading. When a child sees you read, or when you share a book with a child, you're sending a message that reading is important. Show the child that reading a book together is important to you. Find a comfortable, quiet place. Turn off the television and limit other distractions, such as telephone calls.

Be prepared to start slowly. Take turns reading parts of this book. Stop and talk about what you're reading. Talk about the photographs. You may find that much of the shared time is spent discussing just a few pages. This discussion time is valuable for both of you, so don't move through the book too quickly. If the child begins to lose interest, stop reading. Continue sharing the book at another time. When you do pick up the book again, be sure to revisit the parts you have already read. Most importantly, enjoy the book!

Be a Vocabulary Detective

You will find a word list on page 5. Words selected for this list are important to the understanding of the topic of this book. Encourage the child to be a word detective and search for the words as you read the book together. Talk about what the words mean and how they are used in the sentence. Do any of these words have more than one meaning? You will find these words defined in a glossary on page 47.

What about Questions?

Use questions to make sure the child understands the information in this book. Here are some suggestions:

> Where does the saguaro cactus grow? How is the desert similar to our neighborhood and how is it different? What would you need to live in the desert? How is the cactus different from the plants we have in our yard? How is it similar? Why is the cactus so different from other plants? Why doesn't a cactus have leaves? Why does it have spines? Name other plants and animals that live with saguaros. How do saguaros make seeds?

If the child has questions, don't hesitate to respond with questions of your own like: What do *you* think? Why? What is it that you don't know? If the child can't remember certain facts, turn to the index.

Introducing the Index

The index is an important learning tool. It helps readers get information quickly without searching throughout the whole book. Turn to the index on page 48. Choose an entry, such as *seeds,* and ask the child to use the index to find out how seeds sprout. Repeat this exercise with as many entries as you like. Ask the child to point out the differences between an index and a glossary. (The index helps readers find information quickly, while the glossary tells readers what words mean.)

All the World in Metric!

Although our monetary system is in metric units (based on multiples of 10), the United States is one of the few countries in the world that does not use the metric system of measurement. Here are some conversion activities you and the child can do using a calculator:

WHEN YOU KNOW:	MULTIPLY BY:	TO FIND:
miles	1.609	kilometers
feet	0.3048	meters
inches	2.54	centimeters
gallons	3.787	liters
tons	0.907	metric tons
pounds	0.454	kilograms

Activities

Imagine being a saguaro cactus. How is a saguaro like you and how is it different?

Compare a cactus to an ivy plant. Where is food made in the ivy? Where does the cactus make its food? How are the roots alike and how are they different?

Use a plastic bag to cover the parts of the cactus and ivy that are above the soil. Secure the bag around each plant with string. Put both plants in indirect sunlight for four days. What happened in each plastic bag? (This experiment demonstrates transpiration.) Now put the plant in direct sunlight for four days. What has happened? Which plant has lost more water? Why? Why does the cactus do so well in the desert?

Visit a public garden that has a cactus display. Compare the different types of cactuses.

Glossary

carbon dioxide (dy-AHK-side)—a gas in the air that is taken in by plants and used to make food

chlorophyll (KLOR-uh-fihl)—the green color in a plant's leaves or stem that makes photosynthesis possible

nectar—a sweet liquid in flowers that attracts insects, birds, and bats

oxygen (AHKS-uh-jehn)—a gas that plants give off to the air during transpiration

photosynthesis (foh-toh-SIHN-thuh-sihs)—the way green plants use the energy from sunlight to make food out of carbon dioxide and water

pleats—parts of a saguaro's stem that store water

pollen—yellow dust from a flower that is needed to make seeds

pollinating (PAHL-uh-nay-ting)—carrying pollen from one flower to another so seeds can form

seedling—a young plant

sprout—to begin to grow

succulents (SUHK-yuh-lehnt)—plants with special roots, stems, or leaves that store water

transpiration (trans-puh-RAY-shun)—the giving off of water from a green plant's leaves or stem

Index